Take Home Skill-Builders
for Winter

Activities That Involve School, Parents and Child

Written by Ann Richmond Fisher

Illustrated by Ron Wheeler

Teaching & Learning Company

1204 Buchanan St., P.O. Box 10
Carthage, IL 62321-0010

This book belongs to

_____

Cover paper sculpture by Gary Hoover

Cover photo by Images and More Photography

Copyright © 1998, Teaching & Learning Company

ISBN No. 1-57310-118-4

Printing No. 987654321

Teaching & Learning Company
1204 Buchanan St., P.O. Box 10
Carthage, IL 62321-0010

Table of Contents

Dear Teacher or Parent,

Take Home Skill-Builders for Winter is a wonderful collection of family homework activities for early learners. This book provides the classroom teacher with a fun way to involve the students' families in the learning process. The family "helper" will not be just a silent observer but an active participant in the pages that follow. And we guarantee that the activities are "family friendly"—not too lengthy or difficult to put off parents! Students will have fun practicing important skills with the help of someone very important at home.

This book is also "teacher friendly," containing everything you will need to make this project successful. There is a reproducible letter that will explain the *Take-Home* idea to families, a table of contents to help you locate material quickly and a brief answer key in the back for selected activities. In addition, each activity is clearly labeled with the featured skill and the seasonal date to which it corresponds.

Activities are arranged chronologically throughout the winter season. There are general monthly pages, general winter pages, as well as activities for specific special days such as Christmas, Hanukkah, Clean Off Your Desk Day, Presidents' Day and many more. Usually the easier pages in each section appear first.

Skills covered include the alphabet, numbers, beginning sounds, spelling, vocabulary, arithmetic, geometry, history, geography, following directions, noting details and many more. For each month of winter you will find several appropriate and important skills for any primary class. You will notice that on some pages the directions seem a bit difficult for young students. That is where the family helper can be called upon. There are also extension activities on many pages that allow the student and helper to "personalize" the exercise, to discuss the topic further, or to work a little harder. You may wish to make these optional at times.

Best wishes for an exciting winter as your students, and their families, dive into these *Take Home Skill-Builders for Winter!*

Sincerely,

Ann

Ann Richmond Fisher

Dear Family,

This winter our class will be working on some *Take Home Skill-Builders.* These are short, interesting activities that your child will be asked to complete at home with the help of someone in your family. I hope that you and your child will spend a few enjoyable minutes together completing each one that is sent home.

There will be a wide range of activities including word puzzles, coloring pages, math fun and much more. Often there is a related topic for family discussion. The purpose of these assignments is three-fold:

1. to have your child practice the skill featured on each page
2. to teach responsibility of taking the page home, completing it and returning it on time
3. to involve the family in your child's schoolwork

You can help your child by reading the directions together, discussing possible solutions and helping him or her to neatly supply the solutions. Some pages will require more of your help than others. Each page includes a due date and a place for your signature. Occasionally you may need a dictionary, atlas or some other reference book to help you complete a page. If these aids are not available in your home, just do your best.

I trust that you will find many enjoyable activities coming to your home this winter. Please encourage your child to complete each one, if at all possible. Thank you in advance for your support and participation. I value your time and your input, and your child will, too!

Sincerely,

Teacher

D-D-December!

December brings the beginning of winter and the end of the year. You can hear the *D* sound in either the beginning or the end of each picture word below. If the *D* sound comes at the beginning of the word, color the picture. If the *D* sound comes at the end of the word, underline the picture.

With your family helper, make a short list on the back of this sheet of things around your house that begin or end with the *D* sound.

Due: _____

Helper: _____

December

With your family helper, complete this calendar for December of this year. Fill in the missing letters in the month, the missing year, the missing letters in the days of the week and all the dates.

D CE B R						_____ year
unday	onday	uesday	ednesday	ursday	riday	aturday

Find a good place at home to hang the calendar so you can look at it every day.

Before you copy this to give to your students, be sure to write down any school holidays or special events for that month.

Helper: _____

Due: _____

Orderly Months

You probably already know that December is the last month of the year. How well do you know the order of the other months? Number these months from 1 to 12 to show the order in which they come during the year.

Skill

Months of the Year

_____ March

_____ December

_____ February

_____ July

_____ April

_____ October

_____ January

_____ November

_____ August

_____ September

_____ June

_____ May

December

General

Talk with your favorite family helper about which is your favorite month and why.

Due: _____

Helper: _____

Five-Letter Bingo

Here is a bingo card that has letters in all the boxes instead of numbers. How many five-letter words can you find on this card? Look for five letters in a row going forwards, down or diagonally that spell a common word. Write the words that you find on the lines.

_____

_____

_____

_____

_____

B	I	N	G	O
M	E	T	A	L
A	A	H	G	L
R	R	E	A	A
C	L	A	I	M
H	Y	E	N	A

Fill in the bingo card below and hide your own five-letter words. Can your family helper find them?

December

Bingo's
Birthday
Month

Helper: _____   Due: _____

Bingo Clues

Skill

Even/odd, greater/less than

This bingo card is missing a few numbers. Use the clues to find out what they are, and write the numbers in the empty spaces. Remember that the numbers shown under each letter are the lowest and highest numbers that can go in each column.

1. The B numbers are all even numbers.
2. The missing B number is greater than any of the other B numbers shown.
3. The missing I number is less than any of the numbers shown.
4. All the I numbers are odd.
5. The missing N number comes between the two even numbers shown.
6. The missing G number is one greater than the largest odd number shown.
7. The missing O number is less than the smallest even number shown.

B 1-15	I 16-30	N 31-45	G 46-60	O 61-75
10	29		53	67
	23	38	58	70
6	25	FREE		62
12	19	36	55	
8		39	51	64

December

Bingo's
Birthday
Month

Due: _____

Helper: _____

Let's Play Bingo!

In honor of Bingo's birthday in December 1929, three friends are playing the game. Their game cards are shown. A fourth friend, Dean, selects the numbers out of the bag in the order listed. With your family helper, find some markers to keep track of the game. As each number is drawn, mark it whenever it appears on a card. Who is the first person to bingo in each game? Draw a light pencil line through each card that has a bingo.

Game 1

B8, I23, O67, B11, G57, B13, G59, N35, B7, O63, I16, I17

Winner: _____

Everyone clears their card and plays again.

Game 2

B1, O70, N32, B15, G55, N34, B6, O69, I25, G60, G47, B11, I29

Winner: _____

The three friends clear their cards and play one last game.

Game 3

O64, N31, I30, O65, B3, G50, N39, B5, I29, I17, G57, I10, N40, N32, O69, N35

Winner: _____

If you have a bingo set at home, play a game with your family helper.

Rachel

B	I	N	G	O
1	25	39	50	67
11	9	32	57	64
14	23	FREE	49	70
6	29	34	60	69
7	18	35	54	63

Tyson

B	I	N	G	O
8	17	40	57	64
13	24	35	46	70
15	28	FREE	59	62
1	16	31	55	69
5	25	32	50	70

Naomi

B	I	N	G	O
3	22	40	60	67
11	16	34	59	71
15	19	FREE	47	68
5	17	39	51	65
13	30	33	55	74

December

Bingo's Birthday Month

Helper: _____   Due: _____

Capital Directions

December is an important month in U.S. history. It marks the month when Delaware became the first state in 1787. Do you know the name of Delaware's capital city? Follow the directions carefully to find out.

Skill

Following directions

1. First write just the consonants in DELAWARE in order.

    _____

2. Next replace the third consonant from the left with a V.

    _____

3. Now add the letter E between the first and second consonants

    from the right. _____

4. Add the letter O between the second and third consonants from the

    left. _____

5. Finally, remove the third consonant from the right.

    _____

Do you know the capital city of your state? With your family helper, find your state and its capital on a map.

December 7

Delaware became first state

Due: _____

Helper: _____

State Dates

The very first of the 50 United States was Delaware. Listed below are the rest of the 13 original states, in the order in which they were admitted to the Union. Also shown are the dates in which each state was admitted, but these are not in order.

Skill

Putting dates in order

Your job is to put the dates in order from 1 to 13, and then match them with the correct state (the state with the same number) by drawing a line. An example is done for you.

1. Delaware

2. Pennsylvania

3. New Jersey

4. Georgia

5. Connecticut

6. Massachusetts

7. Maryland

8. South Carolina

9. New Hampshire

10. Virginia

11. New York

12. North Carolina

13. Rhode Island

A. February 6, 1788 _____

B. June 25, 1788 _____

C. December 7, 1787 __1__

D. May 29, 1790 _____

E. January 9, 1788 _____

F. December 12, 1787 _____

G. May 23, 1788 _____

H. July 26, 1788 _____

I. December 18, 1787 _____

J. November 21, 1789 _____

K. June 21, 1788 _____

L. April 28, 1788 _____

M. January 2, 1788 _____

December 7

Delaware became first state

With your family helper, try to find each of these states on a U.S. map.

Helper: _____

Due: _____

Fly a Flag!

Around the world, countries work together to protect the rights of all people. Here are the flags of several different countries. Follow the chart to color the flags correctly.

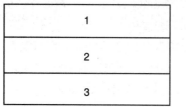

Netherlands

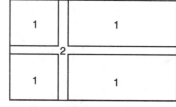

Ireland

1–red
2–white
3–blue
4–yellow
5–green
6–orange
7–black
8–light blue

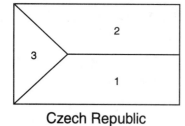

Czech Republic

Denmark

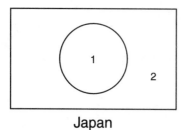

Japan

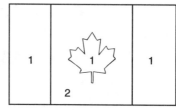

Somalia

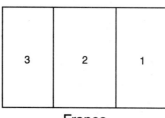

France

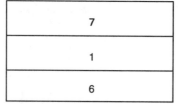

Canada

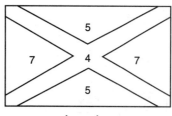

Jamaica

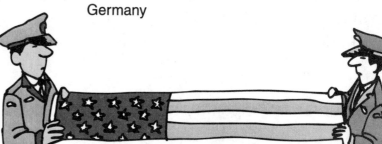

Germany

December 10-16

Human Rights Week

With your family helper, try to find these countries on a globe or world map.

Due: _____

Helper: _____

14

Write About Rights

During Human Rights Week, you may be asked to *write* about human *rights*. The words *write* and *right* are homonyms, words that sound the same but are spelled differently and have different meanings. For each pair of homonyms listed, try to write one sentence that uses both words. Ask your family helper to work with you.

Skill

Homonyms

1. no, know _____

_____

_____

2. pair, pear _____

_____

_____

3. there, their _____

_____

_____

4. to, too _____

_____

_____

5. eight, ate _____

_____

_____

December 10-16

Human Rights Week

List at least 10 more homonym pairs below.

_____

_____

_____

Helper: _____   Due: _____

The Right Country

Human Rights Week is a time for countries all over the world to focus on how people are treated in their land. Some of these world countries are listed below. Can you unscramble each one and write its name correctly on the blank?

1. NAJPA _____

2. DANCAA _____

3. PGYTE _____

4. NACREF _____

5. RASILE _____

6. DEWSEN _____

7. DAINI _____

8. SURAIS _____

9. ZABLIR _____

10. EMICOX _____

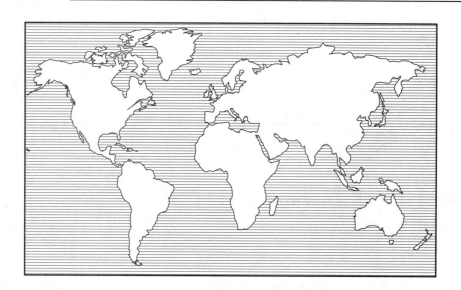

December 10-16

Human Rights Week

With your family helper, locate these countries on the world map. Write the number on the map in the appropriate place.

Helper: _____

Due: _____

Thinking It Over

Many rights are provided for Americans through the Constitution and the Bill of Rights. Some of these are freedom of speech, freedom of religion, privacy and many more. Talk with your family helper about some of these rights. Then think about one of the freedoms that is most important to you.

Skill

Creative writing

What is it? _____

Write three or four sentences about why this is so important.

1. _____

_____

2. _____

_____

3. _____

_____

December 10-16

Human Rights Week

4. _____

_____

Helper: _____   Due: _____

Heads or Tails?

Skill

Addition

Nearly 100 years ago on December 17, two brothers finished building the first airplane. They wanted to take it for a test flight, but they had to decide who would go first. They did this by flipping a coin! Here are some coins that have been flipped a few times, too. Look them over and then answer the questions.

1. What is the value of all the nickels that show tails? _____

2. What is the value of all the dimes that show heads? _____

3. Add together the values of all nickels and pennies, both heads and

   tails. _____

4. Find the value of all the coins showing heads. _____

5. Find the value of all the coins showing tails. _____

December 17

Anniversary of first flight

Due: _____

Helper: _____

Wright Words

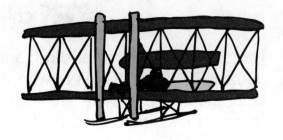

Orville and Wilbur Wright flew the first *airplane* on December 17, 1903. Do you think *anyone* could have been prouder than they when their plane was *airborne* that *afternoon*?

Notice that the four italicized words are all compound words that begin with the letter a. Compound words are made up of two small words. How many can you and your family helper list that begin with each letter below? Try to think of at least one or two for each letter shown.

(Note: Sometimes compounds are written as two separate words, such as *no one* or with a hyphen, such as *blast-off*.)

1. B _____

2. C _____

3. D _____

4. E _____

5. F _____

6. G _____

7. H _____

8. I _____

9. K _____

10. L _____

11. M _____

12. N _____

13. O _____

14. P _____

15. Q _____

16. R _____

17. S _____

18. T _____

19. W _____

20. Y _____

December 17

Anniversary of first flight

Helper: _____   Due: _____

Eight Sets

Hanukkah lasts for eight days, and each box below needs to have eight items in it. Count to see how many are in each box. If there are eight, color the items. If there are more than eight, cross out the extras. If there are less than eight, draw in enough to make eight altogether.

Hanukkah

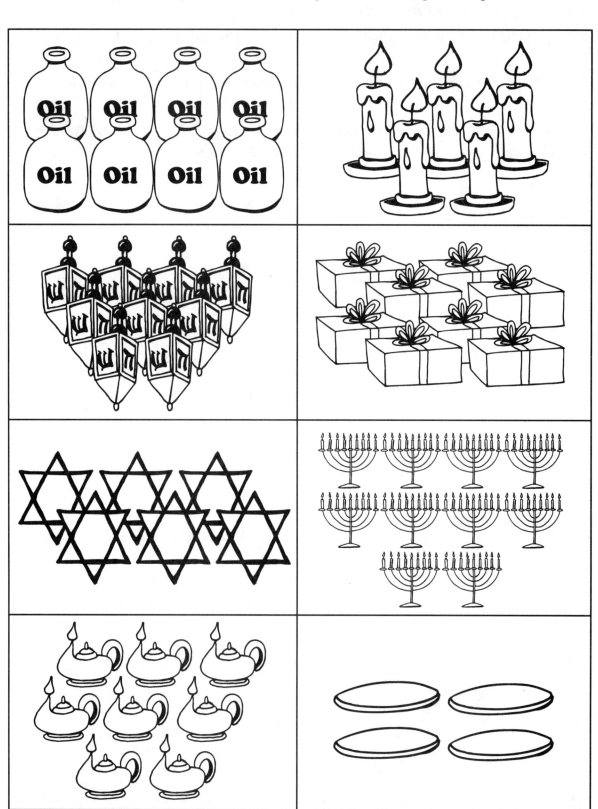

Due: _____

Helper: _____

Star Shapes

The Star of David is an important Jewish symbol, often seen at Hanukkah. Notice that the star is made of two triangles, one placed on top of the other.

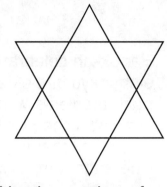

How many triangles are needed to make each shape below? Cut out the triangles at the bottom of the page and try to fit them inside each shape. Write the number of triangles needed on the inside of the shape.

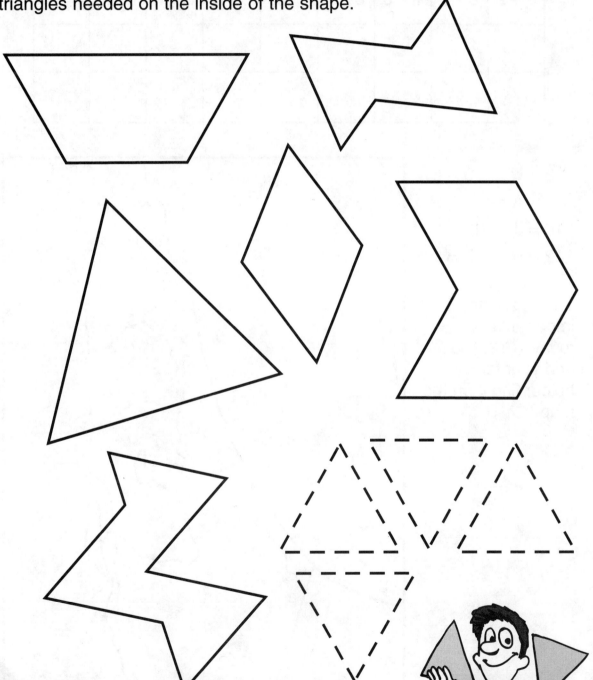

Hanukkah

What other shapes can you and your family helper make with the triangles?

Helper: _____

Due: _____

Eights Are It!

Hanukkah celebrates a miracle when a small amount of oil burned for eight days in the Jewish temple. In honor of those eight days, here are math problems with eights. Write the answer to each one in the first box under the problem. Then find the letter that matches the answer. Write the letter in the bottom box. You will spell the name of the city where the temple was located.

8 + 2	8 - 5	1 + 8	8 - 6	8 + 3	8 - 4	5 + 8	11 - 8	8 + 4

2 = U   3 = E
4 = A   9 = R
10 = J   11 = S
12 = M   13 = L

This is still an important city today. Can you and your family helper find it on the map?

Due: _____

Helper: _____

Gift Giving

Gift giving is a special part of Hanukkah, especially gifts like kindness, friendship and love. Think about a gift you could give to each person below that doesn't cost money. Gifts could include something like helping with a chore, sharing a favorite toy, making a homemade card, etc. Write your ideas on the blanks.

1. your parent _____

2. your grandparent _____

3. your brother or sister _____

4. a neighbor _____

5. a friend _____

6. your teacher _____

7. another special person of your choice _____

Now try to actually give at least a few of the gifts on this list.

Skill

Creative thinking

Hanukkah

Helper: _____ Due: _____

Happy Hanukkah!

You will need some help from your family on this page. First have someone read you this story about Hanukkah. Then together look in the word search for each word that is in bold.

Hanukkah is a **Jewish festival** that happens in **December**, or the **Hebrew** month of **Kislev**. It is also called **Chanukah**, the Festival of **Lights**, the **Feast** of **Dedication** and the Feast of **Maccabees**. The festival marks the day when Jews were able to make the **temple** of **Jerusalem** sacred again after its **recapture** from an **enemy**. A **miracle** is written in the **Talmud**, the Jewish holy **book**, about a day's supply of olive **oil** that burned for **eight days**, until more oil could be brought in. Today the **menorah**, which holds nine **candles** is an important symbol of Hanukkah. The **Star of David** is a familiar **symbol**, too. During the eight days, Jewish children play with a top, or a **dreidel**. They also exchange **gifts** and make **latkes** (**potato pancakes**) which have been fried in oil. This is a reminder of the oil that burned in the temple **lamp** long ago.

Hanukkah

```
L  I  G  H  T  S  N  O  I  T  A  C  I  D  E  D
H  A  R  O  N  E  M  I  R  A  C  L  E  L  O  R
D  I  V  A  D  F  O  R  A  T  S  M  O  G  H  E
E  O  K  I  S  L  E  V  K  O  O  B  L  N  K  I
C  I  P  O  T  A  T  O  D  U  M  L  A  T  M  D
E  L  A  M  P  S  Z  W  E  Y  J  B  T  O  E  E
M  A  C  C  A  B  E  E  S  N  U  Y  K  C  L  L
B  G  F  T  S  A  E  F  P  H  E  V  E  A  A  E
E  Q  T  P  A  N  C  A  K  E  S  M  S  N  S  L
R  E  C  A  P  T  U  R  E  Y  J  I  Y  D  U  P
T  H  R  Y  H  A  K  U  N  A  H  C  W  L  R  M
S  T  F  I  G  S  Y  A  D  T  H  G  I  E  E  E
H  A  N  U  K  K  A  H  E  B  R  E  W  S  J  T
```

Due: _____

Helper: _____

Party Patterns

Here are some strings of Christmas party decorations. Draw the next two items on each string.

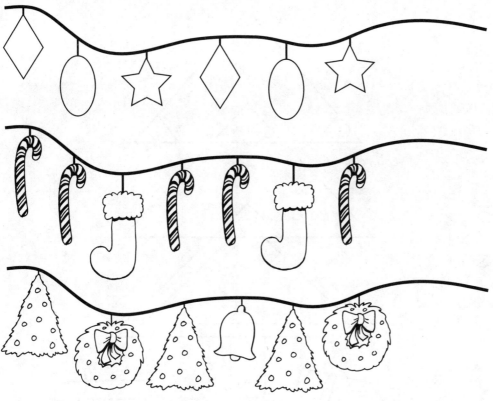

Now get out your crayons and color these strings of Christmas lights as shown. Then color the next two lights to fit each pattern.

1–red   2–green   3–blue   4–yellow

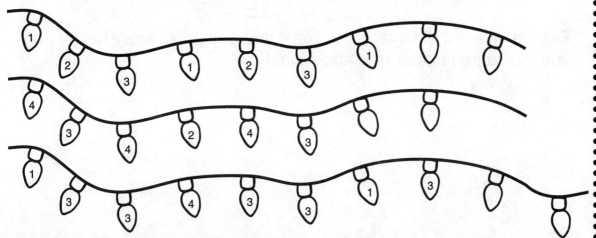

Color your own new pattern on this set of lights. See if your family helper can add two more lights to fit your pattern.

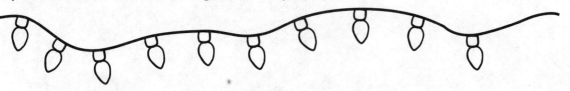

Helper: _____   Due: _____

Triangle Tree

How many triangles can you find in this tree? _____
Color the presents under the tree.

Draw a different triangle tree. See if you and your family helper can find the same number of triangles in it.

**December
25**

Christmas

Due: _____

Helper: _____

Cookie Counting

Paul and Pam have been baking Christmas cookies which are now sitting on a cooling rack. They want to play a little game. Can you help them? Paul cuts out all the stars, and Pam made all of the angels. They are wondering who has the most sets of three-in-a-row. Pam has circled one set of angels. Circle the rest of the angel sets you can find—sets where three angels appear together in a row across, down or diagonally. Then look for sets of stars and count them, also.

Skill

Observation

Pam (angels) has _____ sets.

Paul (stars) has _____ sets.

Who has the most? _____

December 25

Christmas

Helper: _____   Due: _____

Cookie Cutters

These three cookie cutters are laying on top of each other, and they have been sprinkled with letters of the alphabet.

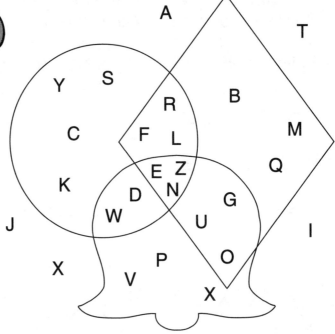

1. What letters are inside the bell? _____

2. What letters are outside the circle? _____

3. What letters are inside the bell and diamond but outside the circle?

_____

4. What letters are inside the circle and diamond but outside the bell?

_____

5. What letters are inside the circle, diamond and bell? _____

6. What letters are inside the circle and bell but outside the diamond?

_____

If possible, help someone in your family bake or decorate Christmas cookies.

Due: _____

Helper: _____

28

Gift Match

Five brothers are each giving their sister a gift. Use the clues to match each boy to the gift he is giving.

Clues	Brothers	Gift
1. Ted's gift is not alive.	Ned	Cactus plant
2. Fred's gift tastes good.	Jed	One dollar bill
3. Ed's gift can be folded.	Ted	Giant candy cane
4. Jed's gift is red and white .	Fred	Gold bracelet
	Ed	Chocolate Santa

Skill
Logic

December 25
Christmas

Talk with your helper about gifts you can make or buy to give to someone else in your family.

Helper: _____

Due: _____

Christmas Pyramid

This food pyramid shows the kinds and amounts of different foods you should be eating every day. For each layer in the pyramid, think of one or two foods you might eat with your Christmas dinner. Write their names or draw their pictures inside the pyramid. Ask your family helper for ideas.

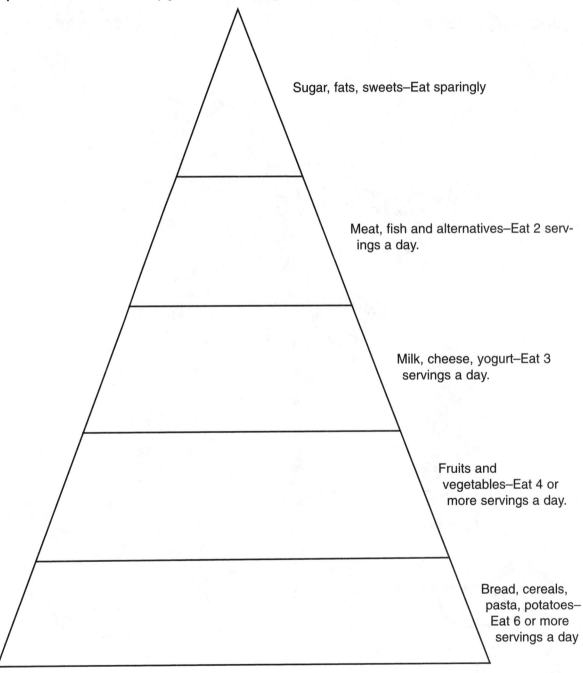

Sugar, fats, sweets—Eat sparingly

Meat, fish and alternatives—Eat 2 servings a day.

Milk, cheese, yogurt—Eat 3 servings a day.

Fruits and vegetables—Eat 4 or more servings a day.

Bread, cereals, pasta, potatoes—Eat 6 or more servings a day

December 25

Christmas

If possible, work with your family helper to plan your meals for one day so that you eat the proper amounts of each kind of food.

Due: _____

Helper: _____

Lick These Problems!

Everyone likes to send and receive Christmas cards. Here is an assortment of postage stamps. Figure out which stamps you need to equal each postal price given. Write the amounts of each kind of stamp needed in the blanks.

 .08

 .60

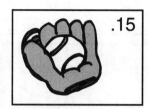 .15

 .21

.32

Example: __37¢—one 21¢ stamp and two 8¢ stamps__ _____

1. 40¢ _____

2. 16¢ _____

3. 75¢ _____

4. 42¢ _____

5. 90¢ _____

6. 29¢ _____

7. 81¢ _____

8. 53¢ _____

9. 23¢ _____

10. $1.00 _____

December 25

Christmas

Work with your family helper to find three new combinations. Then see if you can help someone send their cards by licking stamps, sealing envelopes or signing your name!

Helper: _____   Due: _____

31

January

With your family helper, complete this calendar for January of this year. Fill in the name of the month and the year. Cut out the days of the week from the bottom of the page and glue them in the right spaces. Then add all the dates.

_____   _____ _____
year

Sunday	Monday	Tuesday	Wednesday	Thursday	Friday	Saturday

January

General

Find a good place at home to hang the calendar so you can look at it every day.

Before you copy this to give to your students, be sure to write down any school holidays or special events for that month.

Due: _____

Helper: _____

Soup Cans

Color 1/2 of this can of soup.

Color 1/3 of this can of soup.

Color 1/4 of this can of soup.

Color 1/2 of this can of soup.

January

National Soup
Month

Count the number of soup cans in your family's cupboards. _____

Helper: _____ Due: _____

Soup Ad

What is your favorite kind of soup? Is it sold in the store or does your family make it? Or is it not even invented yet? Think of a good name for your favorite soup, and make an advertisement for it. Include a picture and a tempting description of how it tastes, what's in it, etc.

Ask each member of your family what their favorite kind of soup is.

Due: _____

Helper: _____

Soup Prices

For each pair of soup cans, color the one that is the lower price.

Find out the price of your favorite kind of soup. _____

Helper: _____

Due: _____

35

Constellation Construction

Leo's favorite hobby is astronomy. He loves to look through his telescope and try to find the Big Dipper and other constellations.

Imagine that you have seen these stars in the sky. Use your imagination to "see" a person, animal or object in this group of stars. Draw lines between the stars to make the picture you imagine.

Give the new "constellation" a name. _____

Skill

Creative thinking

January

National Hobby Month

Due: _____

Helper: _____

Puppet Punctuation

Betsy's favorite hobby is writing and performing puppet plays. In honor of National Hobby Month, Betsy has just written a new puppet script. Here are a few lines from it which you need to finish. Add a period to each statement and a question mark to each question.

1. Oh, Ralph, where are you _____

   _____

2. I'm coming, Rosie _____

   _____

3. I was just taking out the trash _____

   _____

4. Is it still snowing outside _____

   _____

5. Should I wear my boots, Ralph _____

   _____

6. Let's go outside and build a snowman, Rosie _____

   _____

With your family helper, write two statements and two questions of your own below.

1. _____

   _____

2. _____

   _____

3. _____

   _____

4. _____

   _____

Helper: _____   Due: _____

Plate Fate

Cleo collects old license plates as a hobby, but she only collects plates that

- have three letters and three numbers
- have numbers with a sum between 10 and 15
- have groups of letters that do not end in a vowel

Circle the plates shown here that Cleo could add to her collection.

Skill

Logic

1. ABC-923

2. 817-DEF

3. GHI-704

4. WXZ-067

5. COD-454

6. OPQ-314

7. 147-RS

8. 317-QRS

9. 625-LMN

January

National
Hobby Month

Ask your family helper(s) to tell you about a favorite hobby.

Due: _____

Helper: _____

TLC10118 Copyright © Teaching & Learning Company, Carthage, IL 62321-0010

Domino Math

Derek's favorite hobby is inventing new domino games. Here is his latest. Cut out each set of dominoes and try to place the three pieces in the spaces shown to get a correct math problem. (You will have to turn some pieces around.) Here is an example of a completed problem.

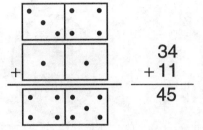

$$\begin{array}{r} 34 \\ +11 \\ \hline 45 \end{array}$$

Skill

Addition, subtraction

Draw your final answer in the spaces.

A.

$+$

B.

$-$

C.

$+$

D.

$-$

January

National
Hobby Month

Enjoy a game of dominoes with your family helper!

Helper: _____

Due: _____

39

New Year's Parties

Ann has planned a lot of activities with her friends for New Year's Day, and they are listed below. Number the events from 1 to 12 to show the order in which Ann should do them.

A. _____ Clean up the kitchen after the party at 6:00 p.m.

B. _____ Vacuum the living room at 10:15 p.m.

C. _____ Be ready to welcome all the party guests at 12:30 p.m.

D. _____ Watch the New Year's Day parade at 11:00 a.m.

E. _____ Start making sandwiches for the party at 9:30 a.m.

F. _____ Go to the neighbor's New Year's party at 7:00 p.m.

G. _____ Get up, shower and eat breakfast at 9:00 a.m.

H. _____ Drive friends back home after the party at 5:30 p.m.

I. _____ Go pick up two friends for the party at 12 noon.

J. _____ Make a fruit salad for the party at 10:00 a.m.

K. _____ Watch a football game with friends at 1:00 p.m.

L. _____ Go snowshoeing with friends at 3:30 p.m.

January 1

New Year's Day

Work with your family helper to write a schedule for yourself or the family for one day.

Due: _____

Helper: _____

Riddled Resolutions

Often people make resolutions, or promises, for the new year. They decide to try to do things to improve their lives. Here are six scrambled resolutions. Write them correctly on the lines. Remember to add punctuation at the end of each sentence.

1. promise exercise I get to more

   _____

2. read I want more to books

   _____

3. try kinder be I will to sister my to little

   _____

4. fruits will eat I vegetables more and

   _____

5. television promise I less to watch

   _____

6. about I to more learn computers want

   _____

Helper: _____   Due: _____

Sense Work

Louis Braille was blinded in an accident when he was only three years old. Later, at the age of 15, he developed a method that helps blind people to read by feeling raised dots on paper. So the sense of *touch* replaces the sense of *sight.* If *you* could not see, which sense would you probably use to identify each of these objects? Talk about it with your family helper, and then write *taste, touch, hear* or *smell* on each blank.

1. _____   2. _____   3. _____   4. _____

January 4

Birthday of Louis Braille

5. _____   6. _____   7. _____   8. _____

Close your eyes or have your family helper blindfold you and then give you a few objects to identify by touch. Don't peek! Is it difficult? Switch places with your helper. Pick new items.

Due: _____

Helper: _____

42

Braille Dots

Louis Braille developed raised dot patterns to represent letters and numbers so that blind people could read by "touch." This activity will help you understand Braille's work.

First draw all the different ways that one dot can appear in this pattern: (The first one is done for you.)

Now draw all the different ways two dots can appear in this pattern:

Now draw all the different ways three dots can appear in this pattern:

The patterns you have just drawn are like those used for the letters A-J and numbers 0-9. There are more spaces and dots used for other letters and symbols.

With your family helper, find the complete Braille alphabet in a dictionary or an encyclopedia.

Helper: _____

January 4

Birthday of Louis Braille

Due: _____

Dream a Dream

In August 1963, Dr. Martin Luther King, Jr. made his famous "I Have a Dream" speech. Talk with your family helper about your dreams for the future. Then together fill in the blanks.

Skill

*Creative
thinking*

I dream that one day I can _____

_____

_____

I dream that one day I will be able to _____

_____

_____

I dream that one day my family will _____

_____

_____

I could help one of these dreams come true by _____

_____

_____

**January
15**

Birthday of
Dr. Martin
Luther King, Jr.

Due: _____

Helper: _____

Map for a March

It is Dr. Martin Luther King, Jr. Day, and your town is organizing a march in his honor. This map shows all the places where the march will go. They must start at city hall, visit each place shown and end at the church. The march must also travel on each road only once.

A. First, use a crayon to draw in a route the march could take. Number the buildings in the order they will be visited.

B. Now measure your route, rounding each line to the nearest inch. Find the total length of your route in inches. Find out how many

feet in all _____.

Skill

Measurement, map scale

City Hall

Shopping Center

Sports Center

Elementary School

Middle School

Church

Library

TV Station

1" (2.5 cm) = 10 feet (3 m)

January 15

Birthday of Dr. Martin Luther King, Jr.

Helper: _____

Due: _____

King's Roles

Dr. Martin Luther King, Jr. did many things in his short life. Find out what some of his roles were by using the code to solve each word.

Skill

Logic

A = H
B = L
C = R
D = N
F = I
G = P
H = T
I = F
J = A
K = S
L = C
M = K
N = W
O = Z
Q = F
R = B
S = D
T = E
W = O
Z = U

1. KGTJMTC _____

2. GJKHWC _____

3. AZKRJDS _____

4. GTJLT GCFOT NFDDTC _____

5. QJHATC _____

6. KHZSTDH _____

7. GTJLTQZB BTJSTC _____

8. KWD _____

January 15

Birthday of Dr. Martin Luther King, Jr.

Due: _____

Helper: _____

Marvin's Mess

Marvin really needs to clean his desk, especially now that it's National Clean Off Your Desk Day. Look at the objects on his desk. What should Marvin throw away? What should he keep? Color the things he should keep. Put a *X* on what he should discard.

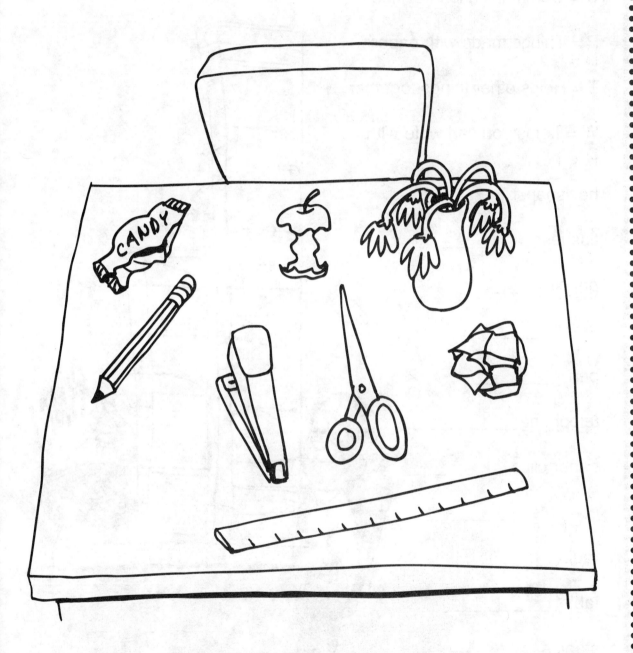

Is there a desk or other place in your room that needs attention? Work with your family helper to clean it.

Helper: _____

Due: _____

Everything in Its Place

Each of these desktop items can fit into one of the groups shown. Read through the list with your family helper. After each item, write *C*, *P*, *T* or *W* to show in which group each thing belongs.

C = Communication devices

P = Things made with paper

T = Holds other things together

W = Items you can write with

newspaper _____

tissues _____

pencil _____

tape _____

pen _____

telephone _____

paper clips _____

computer _____

radio _____

tablet _____

staples _____

markers _____

Due: _____

Helper: _____

Cleanup Crossword

Nancy has cleaned off her desk and saved several useful items. They are shown below. Find the correct word for each one in the word list, and copy the word into its matching place in the crossword.

Word List

apple	paper	radio	tissues
calendar	paper clips	ruler	tacks
clock	pencil	scissors	telephone
computer	pens	stapler	tape
newspaper			

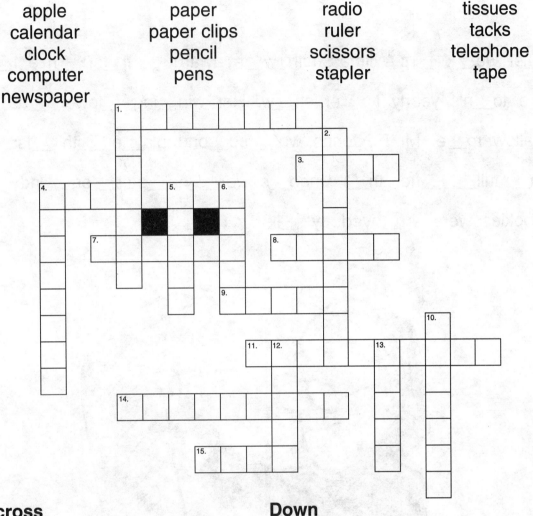

Across

1.

3.

4.

7.

8.

9.

11.

14.

Down

1.

2.

4.

5.

6.

10.

12.

13.

15.

Helper: _____

Due: _____

Printing Problem

One of Benjamin Franklin's first jobs was as a printer. Here is a story that he may have printed long ago in his newspaper. You will see, however, that many of the letters are not yet in place. Fill in each missing letter.

Skill

Spelling, comprehension

L__st we__k __rs. Wilma Smith w__s awarde__ fi__st __rize i__

t__e to__n's yearly flo__er sh__w. Her win__ing __lower __as a

__ellow ro__e. Mr. Ed Jones wo__ se__ond pla__e __ith __is

pin__ tuli__. __fter th__ winne__s wer__ na__ed, __ea __nd

__ookies were en__oyed by __ll.

January 17

Birthday of Benjamin Franklin

Read a newspaper article together with your family helper.

Due: _____

Helper: _____

Franklin's Fractions

Besides his famous experiments with keys and kites, Ben Franklin was interested in many more things. Use the clues to spell the names of things he invented, founded or worked on in his lifetime. An example is completed for you.

1. ³/₄ of NEWT
   ³/₅ of SPACE
   ¹/₂ of PERSON

2. ⁴/₄ of BOOK
   ²/₅ of SHAPE
   ¹/₂ of OPEN

1. __N__ __E__ __W__ __S__ __P__ __A__ __P__ __E__ __R__

2. __ __ __ __ __ __ __ __

3. ³/₄ of COLD
   ³/₃ of LEG
   ¹/₃ of END

4. ²/₃ of LIE
   ³/₅ of BRAIN
   ²/₃ of RYE

3. __ __ __ __ __ __ __

4. __ __ __ __ __ __ __

5. ³/₄ of HOSE
   ³/₅ of PITCH
   ²/₅ of ALONG

6. ⁴/₅ of FIRED
   ³/₄ of COME
   ³/₃ of PAN
   ¹/₃ of YOU

5. __ __ __ __ __ __ __ __

6. __ __ __ __ __ __ __ __ __ __

7. ⁵/₇ of LIGHTLY
   ³/₄ of NINE
   ¹/₂ of GO
   ⁴/₄ of RODS

8. ⁵/₅ of FRANK
   ³/₄ of LINK
   ³/₄ of STOP
   ¹/₂ of VEST

7. __ __ __ __ __ __ __ __ __ __ __ __ __ __

8. __ __ __ __ __ __ __ __ __ __ __ __ __ __

Write a fraction riddle for the names of some fruits. See if your family helper can solve them.

Helper: _____

Due: _____

Scrambled Sayings

Benjamin Franklin was well-known for his sayings, or proverbs, many of which were printed in his *Poor Richard's Almanac*. Read through these proverbs with your family helper and unscramble the bold words. Then discuss the meaning of each of Franklin's sayings.

Skill

*Logic,
comprehension*

1. Be slow in choosing a friend, **lwsore** in changing. _____

2. Whatever **nebigs** in anger, ends in shame. _____

3. Haste makes **stewa**. _____

4. Make haste **wlosyl**. _____

5. Well done is **tebter** than well said. _____

6. You may delay, but **miet** will not. _____

7. **lewl** done is twice done. _____

8. The doors of wisdom are never **tuhs.** _____

9. Early to **deb** and early to **sire** makes a man healthy, wealthy and

swie. _____ _____ _____

Which of the proverbs above is your favorite? _____

Why? _____

_____

_____

_____

**January
17**

Birthday of
Benjamin
Franklin

Due: _____

Helper: _____

Pass the Popcorn!

Five friends are sharing one bag of popcorn for National Popcorn Day. Follow each step below to learn who is holding the bag at the end of all the passing. Look at the clock to help you remember directions.

1. Don starts with the bag.

2. He passes it two places in a clockwise direction.

3. This person passes it four places in a counterclockwise direction.

4. This person passes it three places in a counterclockwise direction.

5. Now this person passes it two places in a clockwise direction.

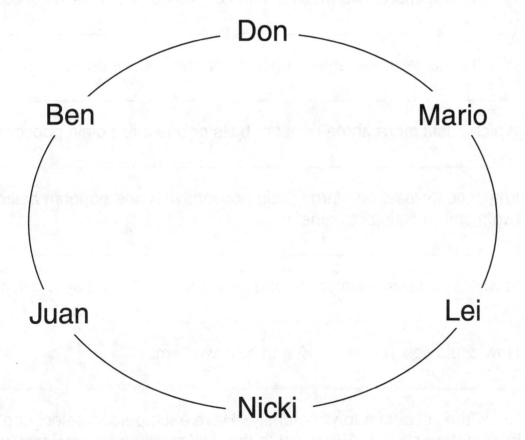

Who ends up with the popcorn? _____

If possible, enjoy some popcorn with your family helper!

Helper: _____

January 22

National Popcorn Day

Due: _____

Movie Munchies

The local theater is selling only popcorn today in honor of National Popcorn Day. Here is a list of their choices and prices:

Small plain popcorn	$.50	Caramel corn	$1.50
Medium plain popcorn	$.80	Cheese corn	$1.25
Large plain popcorn	$1.30	Popcorn ball	$.45

1. What is the most you could spend on one item?

_____

2. What is the least you could spend on one item?

_____

3. Which costs more, two medium plain popcorns or one caramel corn?

_____

4. Which costs less, two small popcorns or one cheese corn?

_____

5. Which costs more, three popcorn balls or one large plain popcorn?

_____

6. Which costs less, one large plain popcorn with one popcorn ball or two medium plain popcorns?

_____

7. In what two ways could you spend less than $1.00 and buy two items?

_____

8. How could you spend $3.00 and buy two items?

_____

9. Show the list above to your family. Have each person select one item of their choice. What would the total price be for your family?

_____

January 22

National Popcorn Day

Due: _____

Helper: _____

Finish the Sentence

Finish each sentence by adding one of the choices given. Then copy the entire sentence again, using your very best handwriting. Finally, draw a picture to go with each sentence on the back.

Skill

Handwriting, sentences

I like to play

in snow.   in the water.   inside.

I would like to visit

a library.   the beach.   the zoo.

I like to eat

an apple.   carrots.   bread.

January 23

National Handwriting Day

Helper: _____

Due: _____

Mirror Writing

Have you ever seen mirror writing? Hold this message up to a mirror. (If you don't have a mirror, you can also turn the paper over, hold it up to the light and look through the paper.)

Can you read this?

Have a nice day.

Here are some letters as they would appear in a mirror. Write each letter in the normal way.

Write a special note to someone in your family, thanking them for something they have done for you. Use your best handwriting.

Due: _____

Helper: _____

Lots of Animals!

Practice your very best handwriting on National Handwriting Day as you spell the plural of each noun. Remember if the word ends in y, you need to change the y to i and add es. If the word ends in x, add es.

Skill

Plurals

dog   dogs   fox

pony   camel

horse   bunny

frog   fly

puppy   cow

zebra   lion

tiger   goat

January 23

National Handwriting Day

Make up a sentence for each plural above. Tell the sentences to your family helper.

Helper: _____

Due: _____

February Finds

How many words can you find spelled with the letters in FEBRUARY? Work with your family helper to spell as many three-letter and four-letter words as possible.

Three-Letter Words	Four-Letter Words
fur	bare
_____	_____
_____	_____
_____	_____
_____	_____
_____	_____
_____	_____
_____	_____
_____	_____
_____	_____
_____	_____
_____	_____
_____	_____

February

General

Due: _____

Helper: _____

February

With your family helper, complete this calendar for February of this year. Fill in the name of the month, the missing year, the missing days of the week and all the dates. Then add these symbols:

♡ for Valentine's Day

🎩 for Presidents' Day

🦫 for Groundhog Day

🎂 for any family birthdays

_ _ _ _ _ _ _ _ _						_____ year
	Monday		Wednesday			Saturday

February
General

Find a good place at home to hang the calendar so you can look at it every day.

Before you copy this to give to your students, be sure to write down any school holidays or special events for that month.

Helper: _____

Due: _____

Mail Sets

The Fisher family has friends and relatives living in many different countries, and they want to send them all some mail during International Friendship Month. For each letter they need one stamp, one airmail sticker, one sheet of paper and one envelope. First of all count the supplies to see how many complete sets they have. Then circle the items they will actually use. (There will be extras of some things.)

Skill

Counting, sorting

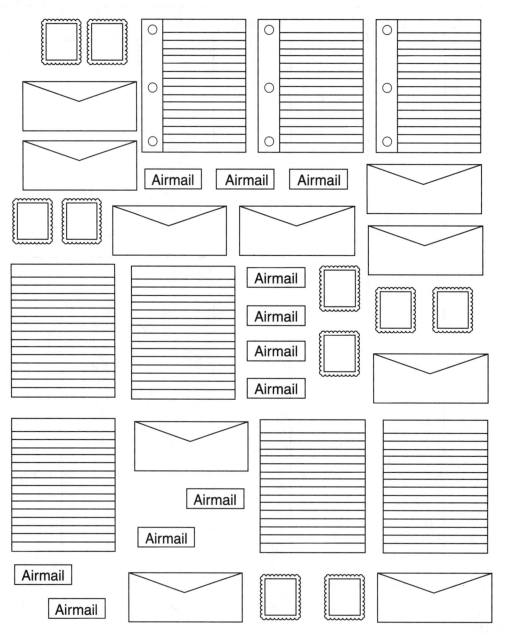

February

International
Friendship
Month

With your family helper, write a letter to someone you know in another country.

Due: _____

Helper: _____

Postcard Pals

Draw a picture on this postcard that could be sent to someone your age living in another country. Think about a picture that will tell this person something about you or about the area in which you live.

Skill

Creative thinking

Now write a brief message to a new friend on the back of the postcard. (Your family may write your message if you wish.)

February

International Friendship Month

Helper: _____ Due: _____

61

Letter Lines

Here is a letter that Rosa wrote to her pen pal in Ireland. You will see that she wrote a very good letter, but she needs to go back and make some corrections. Find the mistakes she made with spelling, capital letters and punctuation and circle them.

123 grand avenue

south bend, IN 46618

february 4, 1996

Deer trudy,

How are you? Im fine. the weather hear in Indiana is still cold ans snowy, but soon it shuld be spring. What is it like in Ireland

Last weak was my birthdy. I had a partie with for of my friends. We went swimmin at a pool. It was fun. My dad gave me a puppy. I named him Sam he is my vary first pet!

Write back soon I always injoy your letters.

Sincerely,

Rosa

February

International
Friendship
Month

Due: _____

Helper: _____

Where in the World?

Mrs. Friend's second grade students have pen pals spread throughout 12 different countries on five different continents. Can you and your family helper figure out on which continent each country is located? Look at a world map or globe for help, if possible. Write the letter for the correct continent in each blank.

1. Mexico_____

2. India _____

3. France_____

4. Nigeria_____

5. Ethiopia _____

6. China _____

7. Peru_____

8. Italy _____

9. Spain _____

10. Canada _____

11. Brazil _____

12. Zaire _____

A–North America   B–South America   C–Europe

D–Asia   E–Africa

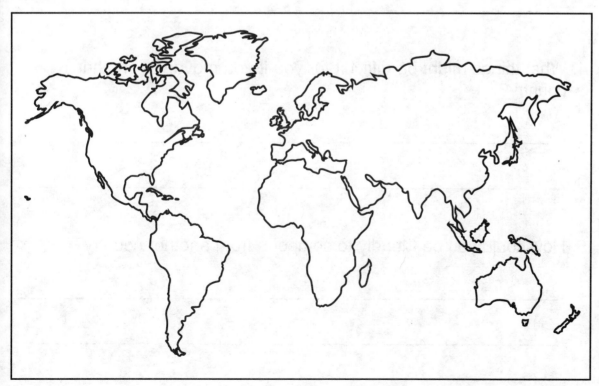

February

International
Friendship
Month

Helper: _____   Due: _____

Friendly Matters

Think about your own friends as you answer these questions. Your family helper may do some of the writing if you wish.

Skill

Creative writing

1. What do you like to do with your friends?

_____

_____

2. What makes a good friend?

_____

_____

3. How can you show your friends you care about them?

_____

_____

4. What things might be difficult for you if you moved to another country?

_____

_____

February

International Friendship Month

5. How could you be friendly to someone from another country?

_____

_____

Due: _____

Helper: _____

Sports Heroes

The drawings below give clues to the names of famous African American athletes. Work with your family helper to solve each one. Write the person's name in the first blank. Write their sport in the second blank.

1.  + E

   _____ _____

2.

   _____ _____

3.  + L

   J + + DAN

   _____ _____

4.  + REE

   _____ _____

5.  + E

   _____ _____

How many other famous African American athletes can you name?

Skill

Solving a rebus

February

Black History Month

Helper: _____   Due: _____

Equal Rights

Black History Month is a good time to remember how hard African Americans have worked to be treated equally. It is also a good time to check your knowledge of words and spelling! See how many words you can spell with the letters in EQUAL RIGHTS. (Watch out–there are oodles!)

Three-Letter Words

sit _____

_____

_____

_____

_____

_____

_____

Four-Letter Words

salt _____

_____

_____

_____

_____

_____

_____

Five-Letter Words

quiet _____

_____

_____

_____

_____

_____

_____

Longer Words

slight _____

_____

_____

_____

_____

_____

_____

February

Black History
Month

Due: _____

Helper: _____

66

Fruit or Vegetable?

A healthy diet includes lots of fresh fruits and vegetables. Color the fruits shown here. Underline the vegetables.

How many more fruits and vegetables can you name? Make a list with your family helper on the back.

Helper: _____

Due: _____

67

Parts Puzzler

It is American Health Month, which is a good time for your body to have a checkup with your family doctor. Here is a checkup for your brain–to see how well you know the parts of your body! In each word below, change just one letter to spell a body part. You will not need to change the order of the letters.

1. train _____

2. root _____

3. pair _____

4. bib _____

5. art _____

6. south _____

7. heard _____

8. sand _____

9. sack _____

10. long _____

11. liter _____

12. gone _____

Due: _____

Helper: _____

Cross-Out

A well-known saying is hidden in the chart below. Uncover it by carefully following the directions below. It is good advice for American Health Month and every other month, too!

	A	B	C	D	E
1	the	an	happy	some	apple
2	a	from	day	with	pear
3	keeps	busy	peach	gum	that
4	but	the	way	water	doctor
5	four	healthy	one	away	end

1. Cross out all five-letter words in column C.

2. Cross out all words beginning with a w in row 4.

3. In column E, cross out all words with less than five letters.

4. In row 5, cross out all the number words.

5. In column B, cross out all the words with more than three letters.

6. In row 2, cross out any words that contain the letter i.

7. Cross out all three-letter words in column A.

8. In column D, cross out all words that rhyme with *come*.

Hidden message: _____

Discuss the meaning of this saying with your family helper.

February

American Health Month

Helper: _____

Due: _____

Exercise Addition

Four friends decided to keep track of the amount of time they spend exercising for one week during American Health Month. Find the total time (in minutes) for each one.

1. Mia jumped rope for 20 minutes each day on Monday, Wednesday and Friday. She swam for 30 minutes on Thursday.

   Total: _____

2. Luke played soccer for 30 minutes on both Tuesday and Thursday. On Friday and Saturday he rode his bike 20 minutes each day.

   Total: _____

3. Keeshan went jogging for 20 minutes on Wednesday and Saturday. He cycled for 30 minutes on Friday.

   Total: _____

February

American
Health Month

4. Aimee did folk dancing for 40 minutes on Saturday. On Tuesday and Thursday she played tennis 30 minutes each day.

   Total: _____

Try to keep track of how much time you exercise for one week.

Due: _____

Helper: _____

Groundhog's Getaway

It is February 2, and that means it's time for this groundhog to get up, get outside and look for his shadow. Help him find his way to the top of the burrow by drawing a path through this maze.

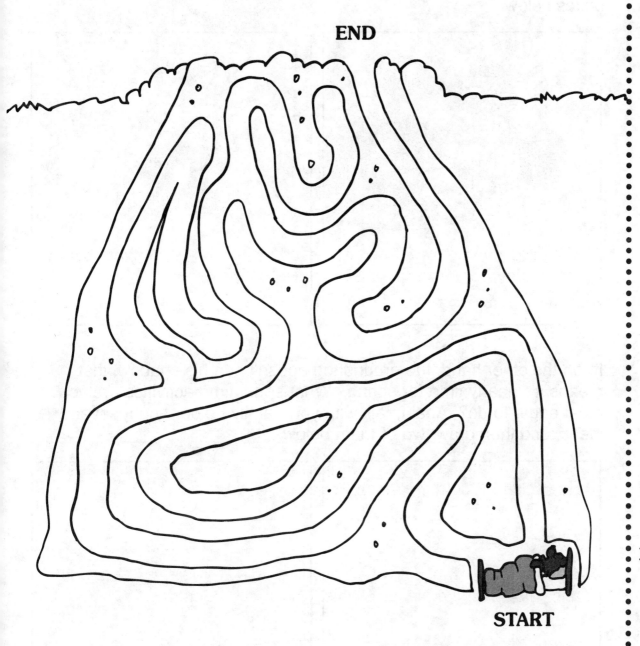

END

START

With your family helper, try to find out more about groundhogs (also known as woodchucks) and their habits.

Helper: _____

Due: _____

Making Plans

February is Groundhog Day and on that day, according to legend, if the groundhog sees his shadow, winter will last six weeks longer. If the groundhog predicts an extended winter this year, what winter activities would you like to do? Talk with your family helper about several ideas, and then draw two of them in the boxes below.

Skill

Creative thinking

If, on the other hand, the groundhog doesn't see his shadow, that means it's nearly time for spring. What springtime activities are you most eager to do? Again, talk with your family helper about several ideas, and then draw two of them below.

February 2

Groundhog Day

Due: _____

Helper: _____

Predictions

On Groundhog Day, people try to predict the weather for the next six weeks. With your family helper, look in the newspaper or listen to the television or radio to learn the weather forecast for this February 2.

What weather is predicted? _____

_____

After Groundhog Day, think about the weather that you actually had on

that day. What was the weather? _____

_____

Was the prediction correct? _____

Do you think a groundhog would have seen his shadow? _____

Why or why not? _____

_____

Now follow the weather predictions in your area for one week. On how

many days was the forecast correct? _____

February 2
Groundhog Day

Helper: _____   Due: _____

Invention Convention

It's Inventors' Day, and almost time for you to take your latest invention to the nearest Invention Convention. Here is a picture of what you have so far, as well as some spare parts which you may or may not need. First, complete the drawing by adding some of the parts shown or different ones of your own. Then give your invention a name. Finally, describe what it can be used for and how it works.

Skill

Creative thinking

Name: _____

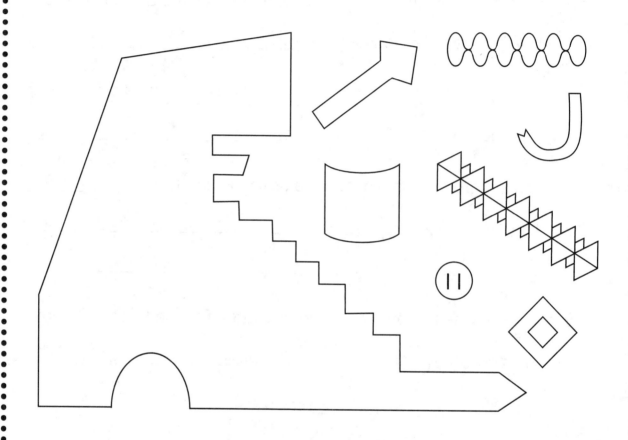

Description: _____
_____
_____
_____
_____
_____
_____

February 11

Edison's Birthday/ Inventors' Day

Due: _____

Helper: _____

Words of the Wise

In 1877 Edison designed the first phonograph, or record player. The first words he recorded and played back were the first line of a famous song. To find out what those words were, cross out every letter of the alphabet in order. Read the letters that remain.

Skill

Creative thinking, logic

ABMCADREYF

_____

GHHAIJD

_____

KALM

_____

NLOITPQTRLSET

_____

UVLWAXYMBZ

_____

February 11

Edison's Birthday/ Inventors' Day

With your family helper, try to learn more about the life of Thomas Edison and his inventions. Write some of your findings on the back.

Helper: _____

Due: _____

Pair Fare

Each valentine card below has a match, except for one. As you find each matching pair, color the two valentines. When you find the remaining single card, circle it.

Helper: _____

Romantic Rhymes

Which valentine word below has the most words that rhyme with it? Make your guess. Then work with your family helper to list as many rhyming words as possible for each. Continue your list on the back if necessary.

Guess: _____

Skill
Rhyming words

LOVE	RED	HEART	SWEET
_____	_____	_____	_____
_____	_____	_____	_____
_____	_____	_____	_____
_____	_____	_____	_____
_____	_____	_____	_____
_____	_____	_____	_____
_____	_____	_____	_____
_____	_____	_____	_____
_____	_____	_____	_____
_____	_____	_____	_____
_____	_____	_____	_____
_____	_____	_____	_____
_____	_____	_____	_____
_____	_____	_____	_____

February 14
Valentine's Day

Helper: _____

Due: _____

Shapely Math

Skill

*Addition,
subtraction,
logic*

1. If ♡ + ☐ = 5, and ♡ - ☐ = 3,

   then ♡ = _____ and ☐ = _____

2. If ⬆ + ◯ = 4, and ⬆ - ◯ = 2,

   then ⬆ = _____ and ◯ = _____

3. If ◇ + 🌷 = 6, and ◇ - 🌷 = 2,

   then ◇ = _____ and 🌷 = _____

4. If △ + ♡ = 7, and △ - ♡ = 7,

   then △ = _____ and ♡ = _____

5. If ☐ + ✿ = 8, and ☐ - ✿ = 2,

   then ☐ = _____ and ✿ = _____

**February
14**

Valentine's
Day

Due: _____

Helper: _____

78

Compound Hearts

Draw a line to connect two heart parts so that they make both a complete heart and a common compound word. Be sure you match the parts.

Skill

Compound words

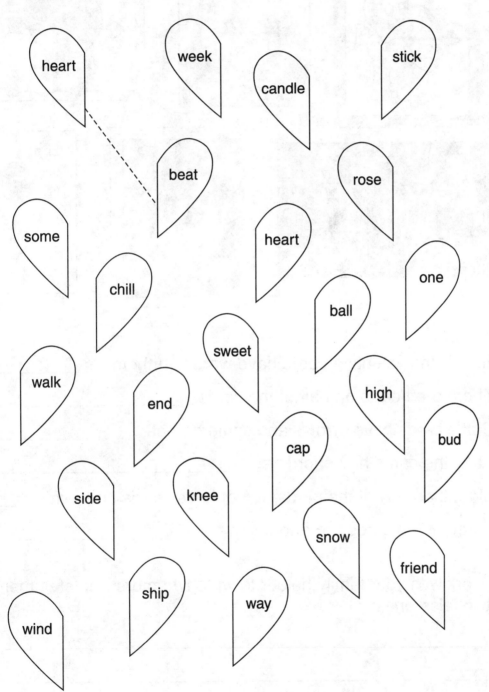

heart

week

candle

stick

beat

rose

some

heart

chill

one

ball

sweet

walk

high

end

bud

cap

side

knee

snow

friend

wind

ship

way

February 14

Valentine's Day

Look around your house for more examples of compound words. Perhaps you will find a *baseball* or a *bookcase*. What else?

Helper: _____

Due: _____

True Love

Study these six valentine cards. Then read the statements below. Write *true* if the sentence is correct, and write *false* if it is not.

Skill

Comprehension

1. Two of the valentine cards have words on them. _____

2. There are hearts on half of the cards. _____

3. Some cards have arrows and some do not. _____

4. All of the cards have borders. _____

5. More than half of the cards do not have words on them. _____

6. Three of the cards are about flowers. _____

Now work with your family helper to write two more true statements and two false ones.

7. _____

8. _____

9. _____

10. _____

February 14

Valentine's Day

Due: _____

Helper: _____

Four for Four

There have been four U.S. Presidents whose last names are spelled with four letters. To find out who they were, write the beginning letter of each picture.

1.

_____ _____ _____ _____

2.

_____ _____ _____ _____

3.

_____ _____ _____ _____

4.

_____ _____ _____ _____

February

Presidents' Day

With your family helper, find out how long ago each of these men were President.

Helper: _____

Due: _____

Presidential Price Tags

Four U.S. Presidents are shown on these coins. Write the value of each coin.

Skill

Coin values

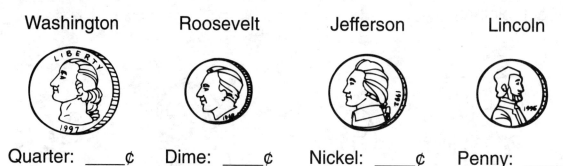

| Washington | Roosevelt | Jefferson | Lincoln |

Quarter: _____ ¢   Dime: _____ ¢   Nickel: _____ ¢   Penny: _____ ¢

Imagine that prices were given by naming the Presidents shown on the coins needed to buy them. Here is an example:

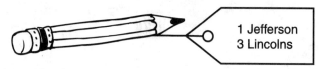

1 Jefferson
3 Lincolns

This pencil would cost 8¢.

Now find the total price for each of these items.

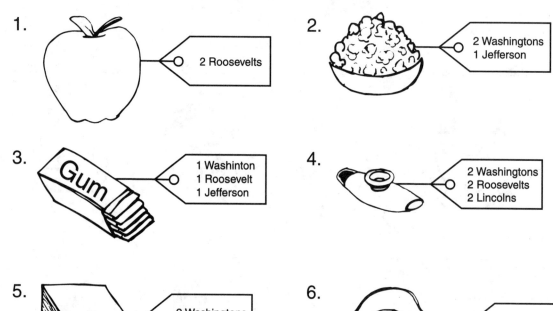

1. 2 Roosevelts

2. 2 Washingtons
   1 Jefferson

3. 1 Washinton
   1 Roosevelt
   1 Jefferson

4. 2 Washingtons
   2 Roosevelts
   2 Lincolns

February

Presidents' Day

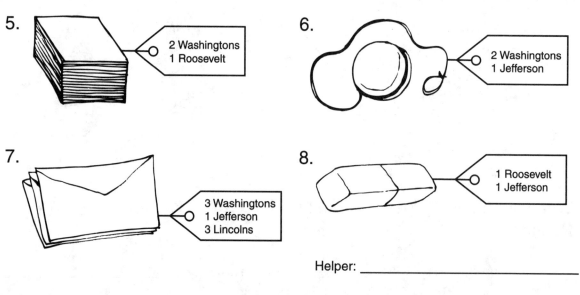

5. 2 Washingtons
   1 Roosevelt

6. 2 Washingtons
   1 Jefferson

7. 3 Washingtons
   1 Jefferson
   3 Lincolns

8. 1 Roosevelt
   1 Jefferson

Due: _____

Helper: _____

82

Top 10

Here is a list of the first 10 Presidents of the United States, along with the year that each one first took office. As you can see, the Presidents are not listed in order. Write the letter for each President in the correct place on the time line to show when each man took office.

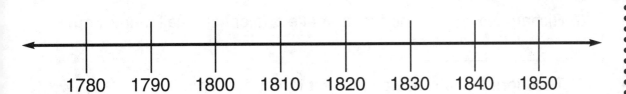

1780   1790   1800   1810   1820   1830   1840   1850

A. James Madison, 1809

B. John Adams, 1797

C. John Quincy Adams, 1825

D. Martin Van Buren, 1837

E. William H. Harrison, 1841

F. George Washington, 1789

G. Andrew Jackson, 1829

H. John Tyler, 1841

I. Thomas Jefferson, 1801

J. James Monroe, 1817

February

Presidents' Day

Ask your family helper who was President when you were born and when they were born.

Helper: _____

Due: _____

Presidential First Facts

Many new things have happened in every President's term. Here are just a few interesting facts. Unscramble the bold words to complete each fact.

Skill

U.S. history

1. Abraham Lincoln was the first President to be shown on a **nico**.

   _____

2. John Adams was the first to live in the **thiwe shoeu**.

   _____ _____

3. Franklin D. Roosevelt was the first to appear on **leviteonsi**.

   _____

4. George Washington was the first President to be shown on a **mptas**.

   _____

5. Grover Cleveland was the first to be **dramire** _____ in the White House.

6. Richard Nixon was the first to make a telephone call to the **onom**.

   _____

7. Theodore Roosevelt was the first to ride in a **rca**.

   _____

8. Woodrow Wilson was the first to speak on the **diroa**.

   _____

9. Abraham Lincoln was also the first President to wear a **drabe**.

   _____

10. John Adams was the first to have a son elected **derspinet**.

    _____

11. Andrew Jackson was the first to be born in a **glo nibac**.

    _____

12. Jimmy Carter was the first President to be born in a **spolitha**.

    _____

February

Presidents'
Day

With your family helper, try to find the years that each man above was President.

Due: _____

Helper: _____

Snowmen

Sam and Sally are twins, and they built twin snowmen. Look carefully at all the snowmen here. Circle the two made by Sam and Sally, the two that are exactly the same.

Winter

If there is snow at your house, try to build a snowman with someone in your family!

Helper: _____

Due: _____

Winter Words

In *winter* and *blizzard* you can hear the short ĭ sound. You can also hear it in words like *ship, fin* and *wig*. Say each word in the diagram aloud to your family helper, and listen carefully to each vowel sound. If the word has the short ĭ sound, color that space. Use the same dark color in all the spaces you color. Then you will have another short ĭ object left in the white spaces.

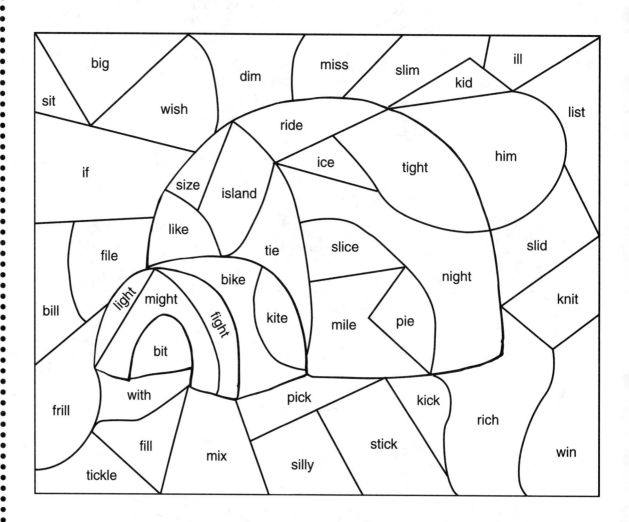

Winter

Look around you to see what other words you and your family helper can find that have the short ĭ sound. Try to list six more words.

_____ _____ _____

_____ _____ _____

Due: _____

North and South

If you live in the Northern Hemisphere, winter comes during the months of December, January and February. But if you live in the Southern Hemisphere, these same months will have warm summer weather.

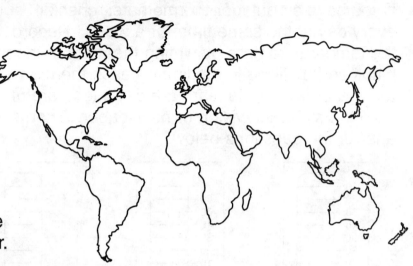

First, draw a dark line with your crayon on the equator, the line that divides the north and south halves of the globe. Color the northern half lightly with your yellow crayon. Color the southern half lightly with a green crayon.

Next, draw a picture in each box to show a Christmas scene for someone living in the Northern Hemisphere (like in the USA or Canada) and then for someone living in the Southern Hemisphere (like in Australia and New Zealand).

Northern Hemisphere	Southern Hemisphere

Winter

If you have a world map or a globe at home, try to find each of these countries with your family helper and tell if they are in a Northern or Southern Hemisphere:

Brazil, Greenland, India, Madagascar, Turkey, Argentina, Ireland

Helper: _____

Due: _____

Temperature Time

If you have an outdoor thermometer, check it every day at the same time for a week. Record the temperature here by writing the number in the blank and by filling in the line on each thermometer. Otherwise, try to learn the day's temperature from the radio, television or newspaper. Then answer the questions below.

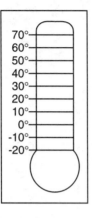

Sunday

_____

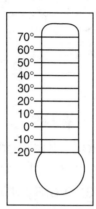

Monday

_____

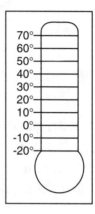

Tuesday

_____

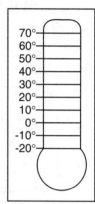

Wednesday

_____

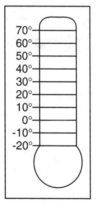

Thursday

_____

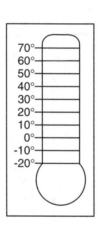

Friday

_____

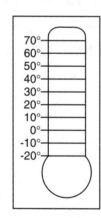

Saturday

_____

Winter

1. Which day showed the highest temperature? _____

2. Which day showed the lowest temperature? _____

3. What was the difference between the highest and lowest

   temperature? _____

Due: _____

Helper: _____

88

Winter Memories

Fold back this paper on the dotted lines so you can see only the top. Study the picture for one minute, trying to remember as many details as possible. Then have your family helper ask you the questions at the bottom of the page. Check your answers together in the picture.

ICE SKATING HERE TODAY
1 p.m. – 5 p.m.
(Closed tomorrow for Christmas.)

FREE HOT CHOCOLATE

1. How many people were in the picture? _____

2. Was it a boy or girl who fell down? _____

3. Was everyone on the ice wearing skates? _____

4. How much did the hot chocolate cost? _____

5. How many cups were on the table? _____

6. How many hours were people allowed to skate? _____

7. What was today's date in the picture? _____

8. How many "buttons" did the snowman have? _____

Helper: _____

Winter

Due: _____

Change-a-Letter

Change one letter at a time to turn SNOW into BOOT and COLD into WIND. The clues should be useful to you and your family helper as you spell each new word. Remember each word has only one letter that's different from the previous word.

SNOW

1. to put into sight

    —— —— —— ——

2. the firing of a gun

    —— —— —— ——

3. black powder from burned coal

    —— —— —— ——

BOOT

COLD

4. fuzzy coating on spoiled food

    —— —— —— ——

5. not very hot, not very cold

    —— —— —— ——

6. part of a human that thinks and feels

    —— —— —— ——

WIND

Now start again with the word *snow*. Work with your family helper to change one letter at a time and make a long list of new words of your own. Try to list 10 or more words. Here is one way you could start: *snow, slow, slot,* etc.

Due: _____

Helper: _____

Sports Reports

One hundred twenty children in one elementary school were asked to name their favorite winter sport. Their answers are shown in this graph.

Read it carefully as you answer the questions below.

1. What sport received the most votes? _____

2. What three sports all received the same number of votes? _____

   _____

3. What two sports together received as many votes as sledding?

   _____

4. Two different groups of three sports each received half of the votes.

   What are the two groups? _____, _____,

   _____ and _____, _____,

   _____.

5. How many more people voted for snowshoeing than ice skating?

   _____

6. Name three sports that together received 50 votes? _____

   _____

7. Which pair of sports received more votes, ice hockey and sledding,

   or snowshoeing and cross-country skiing? _____

8. Which one sport represents 1/4 of all the votes? _____

Take a survey of the people in your family and neighborhood. It can be about their favorite sports, colors, foods, etc. Ask your family helper for ideas. Write the information you find in a chart or graph.

Helper: _____

Due: _____

Zops, Zeps and Zups

Elsie and Eli are playing a winter game with blocks of snow. They have built a lot of different shapes and have given them some unusual names. See if you and your family helper can figure out how their game works.

Skill

Geometry, logic

1. These are called Zops.	These are not Zops.	Circle the Zops here.
		B. C. A. D.

2. These are Zeps.	These are not Zeps.	Circle the Zeps here.
		A. B. C. D.

3. These are Zups.	These are not Zups.	Circle the Zups here.
		A. B. C. D.

Winter

Can you draw three more Zups?

Due: _____

Helper: _____

Answer Key

Bingo Clues, page 10

The missing numbers are B14, I17, N37, G56 and O61

Let's Play Bingo! page 11

Game 1–Naomi, Game 2–Rachel, Game 3–Tyson

Capital Directions, page 12

1. DLWR, 2. DLVR, 3. DLVER, 4. DLOVER, 5. DOVER

State Dates, page 13

1. C, 2. F, 3. I, 4. M, 5. E, 6. A, 7. L, 8. G, 9. K, 10. B, 11. H, 12. J, 13. D

The Right Country, page 16

1. Japan, 2. Canada, 3. Egypt, 4. France, 5. Israel, 6. Sweden, 7. India, 8. Russia, 9. Brazil, 10. Mexico

Heads or Tails? page 18

1. 15¢, 2. 20¢, 3. 24¢, 4. 28¢, 5. 26¢

Wright Words, page 19

Possible answers include:

B–baseball
C–candlestick
D–doghouse
E–everyone
F–farmyard
G–grasshopper
H–halfway
I–ice cream
K–knapsack
L–lighthouse
M–madhouse
N–newspaper
O–outlaw
P–pea pod
Q–quarterback
R–raincoat
S–seesaw
T–takeoff
W–watermelon
Y–yardstick

Eights Are It! page 22

Jerusalem

Happy Hanukkah! page 24

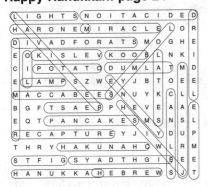

Triangle Tree, page 26

There are 10 triangles in the tree.

Cookie Counting, page 27

Pam has 6 sets; Paul has 4 sets. Pam has the most sets.

Cookie Cutters, page 28

1. D, E, N, W, Z, V, P, O, U, G, X; 2. A, B, M, Q, T, U, G, I, O, P, V, J, X; 3. U, G, O; 4. L, R, F; 5. N, E, Z; 6. D, W

Gift Match, page 29

Ned–Cactus plant, Jed–Giant candy cane, Ted–gold bracelet, Ed–One dollar bill, Fred–Chocolate Santa

Lick These Problems! page 31

1. one 32¢ and one 8¢; 2. two 8¢; 3. one 60¢ and one 15¢; 4. two 21¢; 5. six 15¢; 6. one 21¢ and one 8¢;
7. one 60¢ and one 21¢; 8. one 32¢ and one 21¢; 9. one 15¢ and one 8¢; 10. one 60¢, one 32¢ and one 8¢

Puppet Punctuation, page 37

1. Oh, Ralph, where are you?
2. I'm coming, Rosie.
3. I was just taking out the trash.
4. Is it still snowing outside?
5. Should I wear my boots, Ralph?
6. Let's go outside and build a snowman, Rosie.

Plate Fate, page 38

Cleo should collect plates 1, 4, 5, 8 and 9.

Domino Math, page 39

(Variations are possible.) A. 46 + 20 = 66, B. 54 - 23 = 31, C. 15 + 41 = 56, D. 43 - 22 = 21

New Year's Parties, page 40

A. 10, B. 12, C. 6, D. 4, E. 2, F. 11, G. 1, H. 9, I. 5, J. 3, K. 7, L. 8

Riddle Resolutions, page 41

1. I promise to get more exercise.
2. I want to read more books.
3. I will try to be kinder to my little sister.
4. I will eat more fruits and vegetables.
5. I promise to watch less television.
6. I want to learn more about computers.

Braille Dots, page 43

1 dot:

2 dots:

3 dots:

Map for a March, page 45

One possible route is to start at city hall, go to the sports center, the middle school, the TV station, the library, the elementary school, the shopping center and finally the church. The approximate distance for this route is 15 inches, which converts to 150 feet (1" = 10').

King's Roles, page 46

1. speaker, 2. pastor, 3. husband, 4. Peace Prize winner, 5. father, 6. student, 7. peaceful leader, 8. son

Cleanup Crossword, page 49

Across: 1. scissors, 3. pens, 4. computer, 7. pencil, 8. paper, 9. radio, 11. paper clips, 14. newspaper
Down: 1. stapler, 2. telephone, 4. calendar, 5. tacks, 6. ruler, 10. tissues, 12. apple, 13. clock, 15. tape

Printing Problem, page 50

Last week Mrs. Wilma Smith was awarded first prize in the town's yearly flower show. Her winning flower was a yellow rose. Mr. Ed Jones won second place with his pink tulip. After the winners were named, tea and cookies were enjoyed by all.

Franklin's Fractions, page 51

2. bookshop, 3. college, 4. library, 5. hospital, 6. fire company, 7. lightning rods, 8. Franklin stove

Scrambled Sayings, page 52

1. slower, 2. begins, 3. waste, 4. slowly, 5. better, 6. time, 7. Well, 8. shut, 9. bed, rise, wise

Pass the Popcorn! page 53

Nicki ends up with the bag of popcorn.

Movie Munchies, page 54

1. $1.50 for one caramel corn, 2. 45 cents on one popcorn ball, 3. two medium plain popcorns, 4. two small plain popcorns, 5. three popcorn balls, 6. two medium plain popcorns, 7. two popcorn balls or one small plain popcorn and one popcorn ball, 8. two caramel corns

February Finds, page 58

Possible answers include: three-letter words: ray, rye, far, fry, rub, bar, buy, bay, ear;
four-letter words: bear, fear, fray

Mail Sets, page 60

There are eight complete sets.

Letter Lines, page 62

Dear Trudy,

How are you? I'm fine. The weather here in Indiana is still cold and snowy, but soon it should be spring.
What is it like in Ireland?

Last week was my birthday. I had a party with four of my friends. We went swimming at a pool. It was fun.
My dad gave me a puppy. I named him Sam. He is my very first pet!

Write back soon. I always enjoy your letters.

Sincerely,

Rosa

Where in the World? page 63

1. B, 2. C, 3. D, 4. C, 5. B, 6. C, 7. E, 8. D, 9. A, 10. B, 11. E, 12. E

Sports Heroes, page 65

1. Jackie Robinson–baseball, 2. Tiger Woods–golf, 3. Michael Jordan–basketball, 4. Henry Aaron–baseball,
5. Jackie Joyner-Kersee–track

Equal Rights, page 66

Here are just some of the possibilities:
Three-Letter Words: age, ate, are, ale, art, air, ear, eat, era, gas, hat, her, hit, leg, lit, rag, rat,
    sag, sat, sea, she, sir, tag, tar, the
Four-Letter Words: hail, halt, hate, heat, hear, heal, late, quit, rage, rate, rail, sale, salt, sail,
    seal, star, stir, tail, tale, tear, tire
Five-Letter Words: light, sight, quite, quail, slate, share, shear, shale, heart, earth, stair
Longer Words: square

Parts Puzzler, page 68

1. brain, 2. foot, 3. hair, 4. rib, 5. arm, 6. mouth, 7. heart, 8. hand, 9. back, 10. lung, 11. liver, 12. bone

Cross-Out, page 69

An apple a day keeps the doctor away.

Exercise Addition, page 70

1. 90 minutes, 2. 100 minutes, 3. 70 minutes, 4. 100 minutes

Groundhog's Getaway, page 71

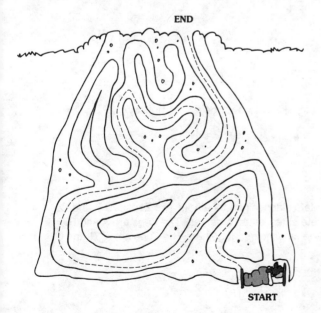

Words of the Wise, page 75

Mary had a little lamb.

Pair Fare, page 76

Shapely Math, page 78

1. ♡ = 4, ▢ = 1;   2. ⬈ = 3, ◯ = 1;   3. ◇ = 4, ⬓ = 2;

4. △ = 7, ♡ = 0;   5. ▯ = 5, ✿ = 3

Compound Hearts, page 79

These words can be made: sweetheart, sidewalk, someone, kneecap, snowball, friendship, candlestick, rosebud, highway, weekend, windchill

True Love, page 80

1. True, 2. True, 3. True, 4. False, 5. True, 6. False

Four for Four, page 81

1. Taft, 2. Bush, 3. Polk, 4. Ford

Presidential Price Tags, page 82

1. 20¢, 2. 55¢, 3. 40¢, 4. 72¢, 5. 60¢, 6. 55¢, 7. 83¢, 8. 15¢

Presidential First Facts, page 84

1. coin, 2. White House, 3. television, 4. stamp, 5. married, 6. moon, 7. car, 8. radio
9. beard, 10. President, 11. log cabin, 12. hospital

Snowmen, page 85

C and G are the same.

Winter Memories, page 89

1. four, 2. girl, 3. no, 4. free, 5. three, 6. four, 7. December 24, 8. four

Change-a-Letter, page 90

1. show, 2. shot, 3. soot, 4. mold, 5. mild, 6. mind

Sports Reports, page 91

1. sledding
2. cross-country skiing, snowshoeing, ice hockey
3. ice skating and downhill skiing
4. downhill skiing, ice skating, sledding and cross-country skiing, snowshoeing, ice hockey
5. five
6. one possible answer: ice skating, downhill skiing and ice hockey
7. ice hockey and sledding
8. sledding

Zops, Zeps and Zups; page 92

1. Zops are shapes built with three cubes, with complete sides joined together. The Zops are B and C.
2. Zeps are shapes built with four cubes, with complete sides joined together. The Zeps are A and B.
3. Zups are shapes built with five cubes, with complete sides joined together. The Zups are A, B and C.